We Are One in Christ

New Tunes for the 21st Century

Tunes by
Carlton R. Young

Texts by
Timothy Dudley-Smith, Heather Murray Elkins,
F. Pratt Green, Fred Kaan, S T Kimbrough, Jr.,
Shirley Erena Murray, Andrew Pratt,
John Thornburg, Thomas Troeger, F. Bland Tucker,
Charles Wesley, John Wesley

Abingdon Press
Nashville

Foreword

Dear Sam (so named as a friend, I would guess, by those of us who are the text writers in this collection, but more formally, Dr. Carlton R. Young).

Are there no bounds to your musical imagination? Charles and John Wesley, F. Bland Tucker, and Fred Pratt Green cannot speak for themselves, but each of us extant have had our words pass your rigorous eye, and have been given your treatment with identifiable flair. Sometimes this is pure simplicity of line, sometimes a musical mischief, often the deep understanding that something different altogether is needed. There is an element of shock implicit in some of your interpretations (see Charles Wesley words in pseudo-Asian mode and John Wesley rocking to gospel), but often we feel we are gathered 'round a keyboard where anything goes if the words have an authentic challenge.

Many of these settings are gracious gifts to friends or tributes to occasions. The phrase "spontaneous combustion" comes to mind when it is obvious what attracted you to an idea. Such feisty immediacy! Your indicators of tempo or style reveal a great deal about your attitude to churchly stuffiness. You give instructions to whistle, or for people to sing while exchanging signs of unity and reconciliation.

And there are further surprises, such as syncopation, jazz chordal structures, calypso, and percussive beat. There is impish imitation of something elusive but eminently singable—musical wit at its best. There is your snippet of AURELIA sliding wickedly, in six flats, into the tune CONCEITED. (I recall that you once interpolated a snatch of "Yankee Doodle" into a hymn on human freedoms.)

This collection dares editorial committees of hymnals to move past the conventional and consider the vital difference made by imaginative harmonization and the element of fun in singing hymns. God laughs when we are so unmitigatedly serious.

Sam, your editorial experience is vast and you have an innate sense of what is singable and sure, in terms of theology. How apt that you have chosen the delightful lines:

> "Be careful what you sing,
> for you may believe it!
> Think carefully what you sing by heart,
> for you may not forget it!"

And, as Don Saliers has written so truly: "Happy the poets upon whose lines Carlton Young's musical eyes and ears focus."

Shirley Erena Murray

Contents

We Are One in Christ

Refrain

We are one in Christ,
and one with each other,
and we are one in ministry to the world.

Refrain

There is one body and one hope,
one Spirit and one call,
one Lord, one faith, one baptism,
and one Parent of us all.

Refrain

Then walk in love as Christ has loved,
who died that he might save;
with kind and gentle hearts forgive
as God in Christ forgave.

Refrain

We are one in Christ.

WORDS: Stanzas by F. Bland Tucker (Eph. 4:1-4)

For Sally Dyck

We Are One in Christ

Hymn Anthem for SATB Choir*, Congregation, Optional Flute, and Keyboard**

*Choral score is printed on page 10.
**Flute part is printed on page 12.

WORDS: Stanzas by F. Bland Tucker (Eph. 4:1-4)
MUSIC: Carlton R. Young

RECONCILIATION
CM with Refrain and Coda

*Congregation may sing melody, or stanzas may be sung by choir alone (see p. 10).

Spir - it and one call, one
died that he might save; with
Dmaj9 Bm/D Em7 F#m7 Gmaj7 G6 Em/G
in tempo
Lord, one faith, one bap - tism, and one
kind and gen - tle hearts for - give as
(+Fl.)
F#7sus F#7 E/F# F#7 Bm Dmaj7/A G A
in tempo

*Choir and congregation sing while exchanging signs of unity and reconcilliation.

**Flute and keyboard improvises on the music provided.

For Sally Dyck

We Are One in Christ

WORDS: Stanzas by F. Bland Tucker (Eph. 4:1-4)
MUSIC: Carlton R. Young

RECONCILIATION
CM with Refrain and Coda

in tempo
1 D.S.
2 D.S.
bap-tism, and one Par-ent of us all.
hearts for-give as God in Christ for - gave.
CODA
Final ending
*
world. We are one in Christ.

For Sally Dyck

We Are One in Christ

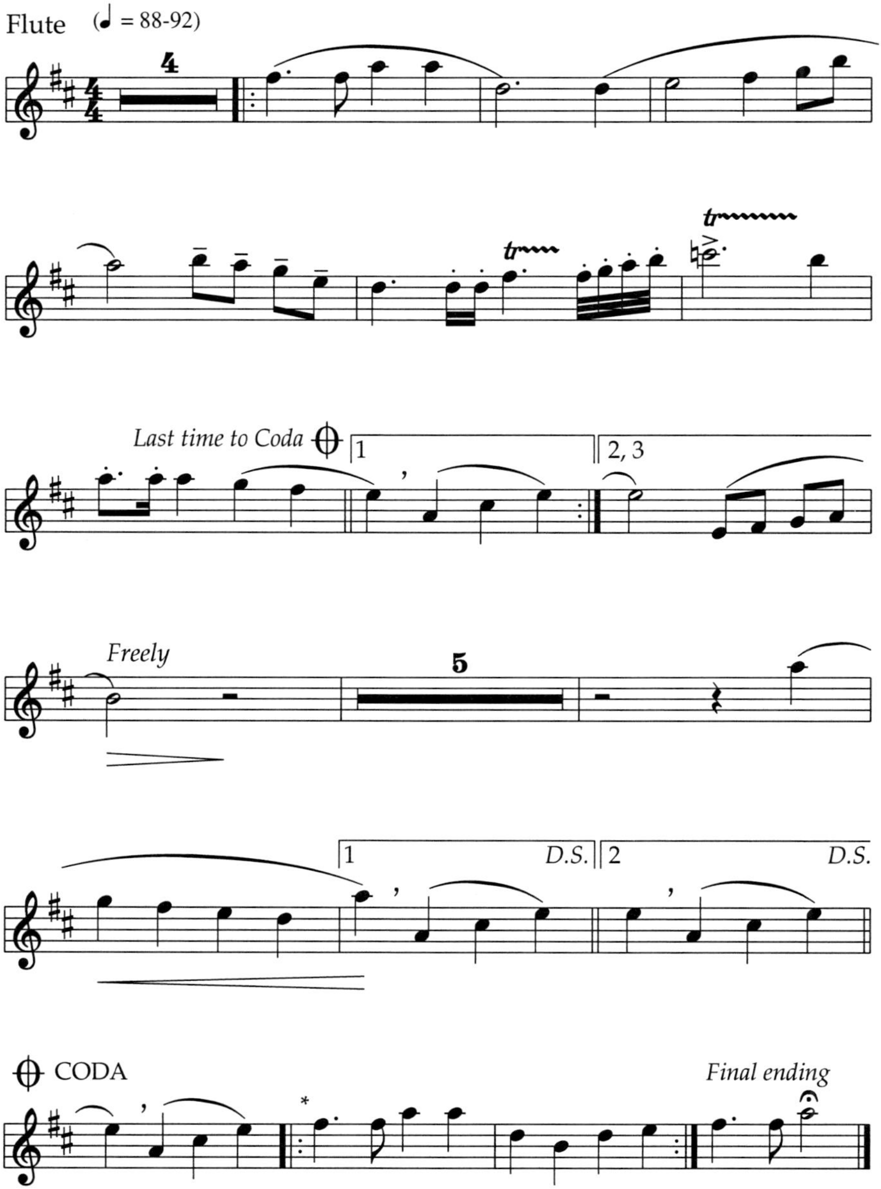

*Flute may improvise on the music provided.

MUSIC: Carlton R. Young

RECONCILIATION
CM with Refrain and Coda

Lord, We Have Your Commission

Lord, we have your commission
to go evangelize
and we know about mission,
we have obtained the prize.
If only others saw things
the way we know they are,
we'd have a world which then brings
uncomplicated war.

Lord, we've heard some are saying
that others globalize,
and that's why we've been praying
help them to rationalize
the things they think they're hearing,
for they don't understand
to wait for your appearing
and then to take a stand.

Lord, we'll pray and get ready,
we'll even sermonize;
for some it may be "heady,"
but we can sanitize
your Word from our perspective,
that's what the world now needs.
For minds still so defective
my view's the truth that leads,
my view's the truth that leads,
my view's the truth that leads.

WORDS: S T Kimbrough, Jr.

Lord, We Have Your Commission

WORDS: S T Kimbrough, Jr.
MUSIC: Carlton R. Young

CONCEITED
86.76.76.76

May be sung SATB using the keyboard harmony.

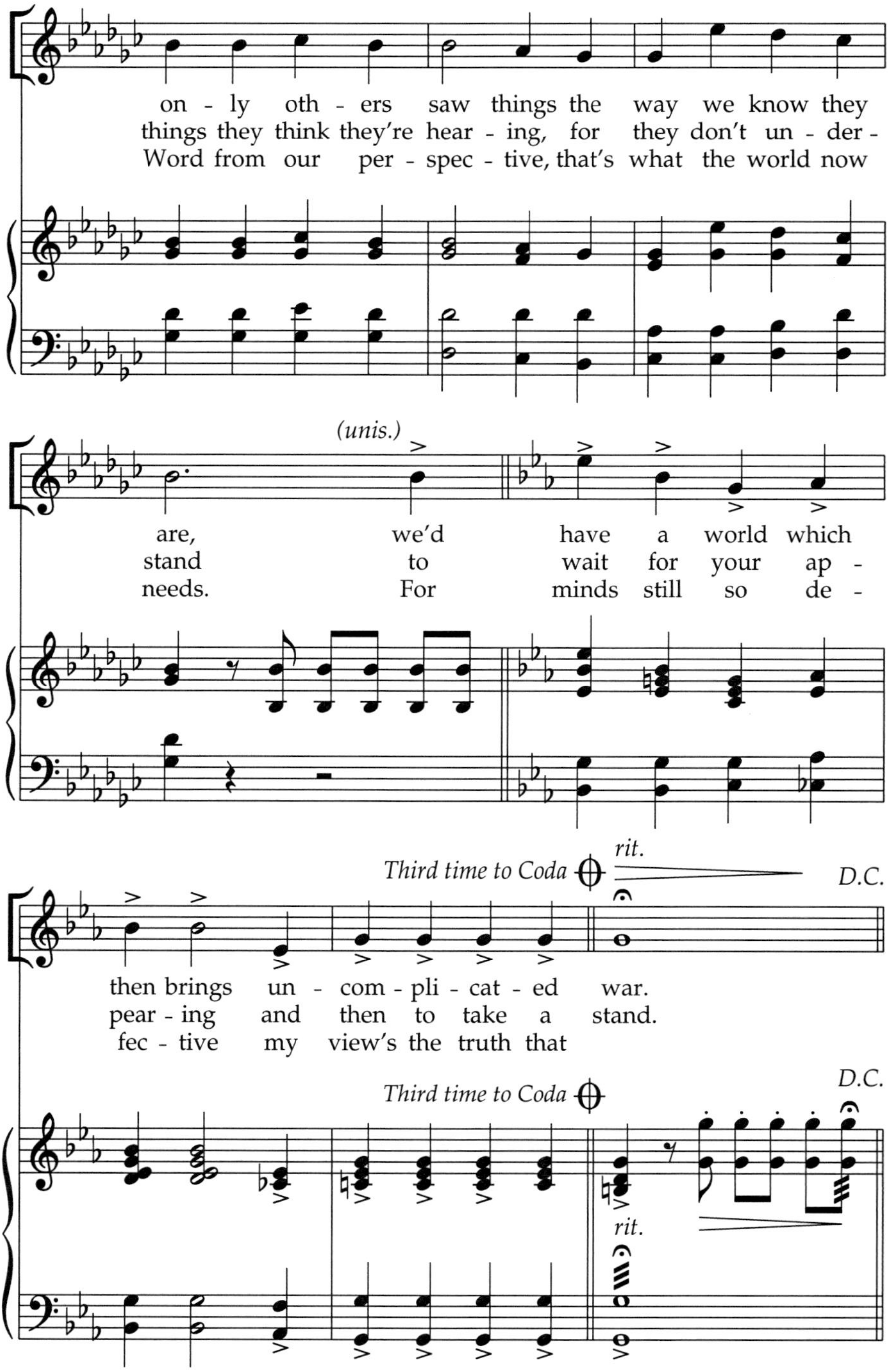
on - ly oth - ers saw things the way we know they
things they think they're hear - ing, for they don't un - der -
Word from our per - spec - tive, that's what the world now
(unis.)
are, we'd have a world which
stand to wait for your ap -
needs. For minds still so de -
Third time to Coda
rit.
D.C.
then brings un - com - pli - cat - ed war.
pear - ing and then to take a stand.
fec - tive my view's the truth that
Third time to Coda
D.C.
rit.

CODA
leads, my view's the truth that leads, my
CODA
view's the truth that leads.
Whistle
repeat as desired
repeat as desired

Lord, We Have Your Commission

May be sung SATB using the keyboard harmony

WORDS: S T Kimbrough, Jr.
MUSIC: Carlton R. Young

CONCEITED
86.76.76.76

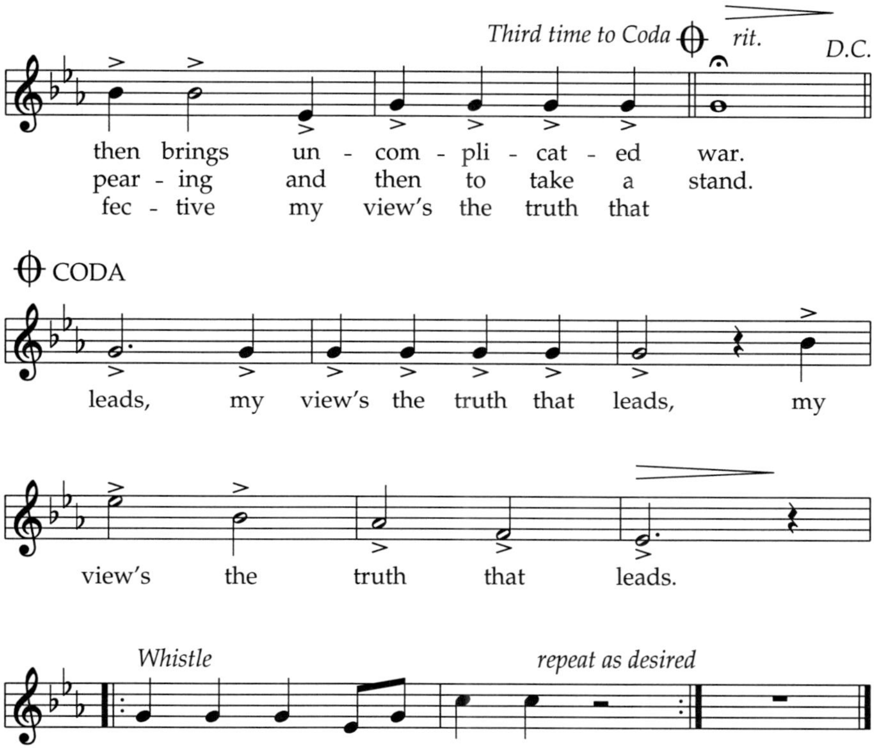
Third time to Coda
rit.
D.C.
then brings un - com - pli - cat - ed war.
pear - ing and then to take a stand.
fec - tive my view's the truth that
CODA
leads, my view's the truth that leads, my
view's the truth that leads.
Whistle
repeat as desired

Take a Tune

Take a tune, make mysteries friendly
play the music of your heart,
reach within each treasured memory
cultivate your precious art.

All your saying, feeling, seeing,
all your history, where you home,
make a context for your singing,
give a sense of what you own.

Never lose your past tradition,
never lose your sense of place,
yet, this is no contradiction,
find new signs of love and grace.

In the essence of your music,
Christ, the starting point of song,
brings new fragrance to each meeting,
helps us all to love along.

WORDS: Andrew Pratt

Take a Tune

WORDS: Andrew Pratt
MUSIC: Carlton R. Young

HEART-BEAT
CM

Take a Tune

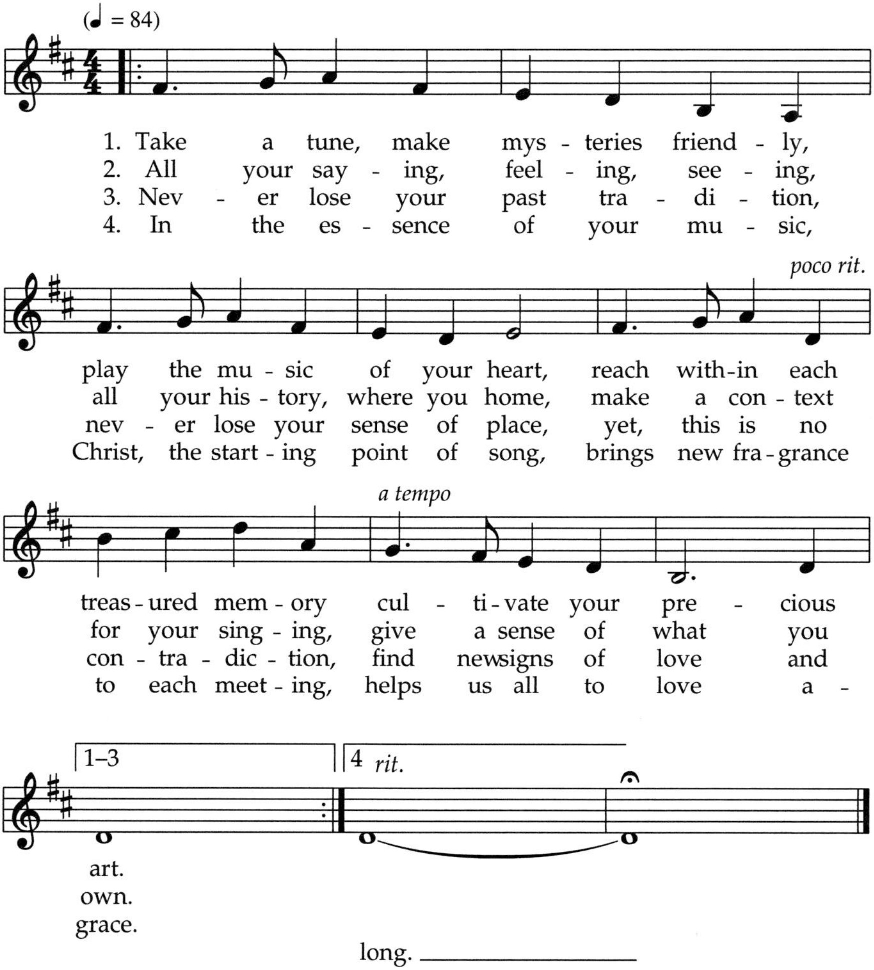

WORDS: Andrew Pratt
MUSIC: Carlton R. Young

HEART-BEAT
CM

Lord and Father, Faith Bestowing

Lord and Father, faith bestowing,
to our hearts draw near.
Love is ours beyond our knowing,
God is here.

Christ our Savior come with blessing,
bid our doubting cease.
Here may all, their sin confessing,
find your peace.

Holy Spirit, life instilling,
breathe from God above;
come with power, our spirits filling,
come with love.

God eternal, grace unbounded,
Three-in-One we praise;
keep us by your love surrounded
all our days.

WORDS: Timothy Dudley-Smith

For Timothy Dudley-Smith, on his 80th birthday

Lord and Father, Faith Bestowing

WORDS: Timothy Dudley-Smith
MUSIC: Carlton R. Young

TIM
85.83

For Timothy Dudley-Smith, on his 80th birthday

Lord and Father, Faith Bestowing

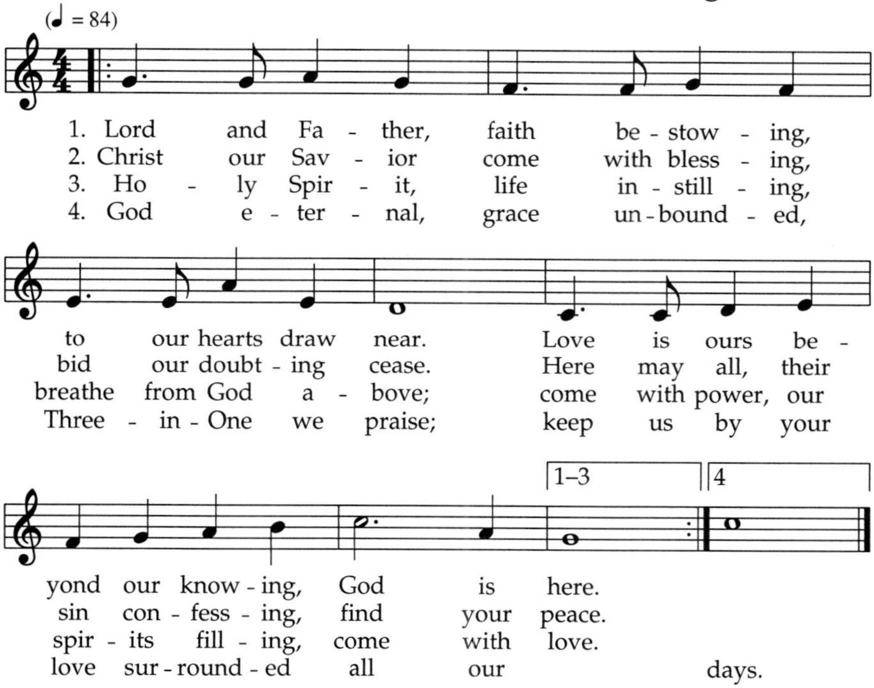

WORDS: Timothy Dudley-Smith
MUSIC: Carlton R. Young

TIM
85.83

Let Our Earth Be Peaceful

Let our earth be peaceful,
let our hearts be hopeful,
let our hands be gentle
for the love of God.

Let our ways be mindful,
mending what is hurtful,
doing what is needful
for the love of God.

Let our lives be fruitful,
beautiful and playful,
every day be thankful
for the love of God.

WORDS: Shirley Erena Murray

Let Our Earth Be Peaceful

WORDS: Shirley Erena Murray
MUSIC: Carlton R. Young

RAYMOND
66.65

Let Our Earth Be Peaceful

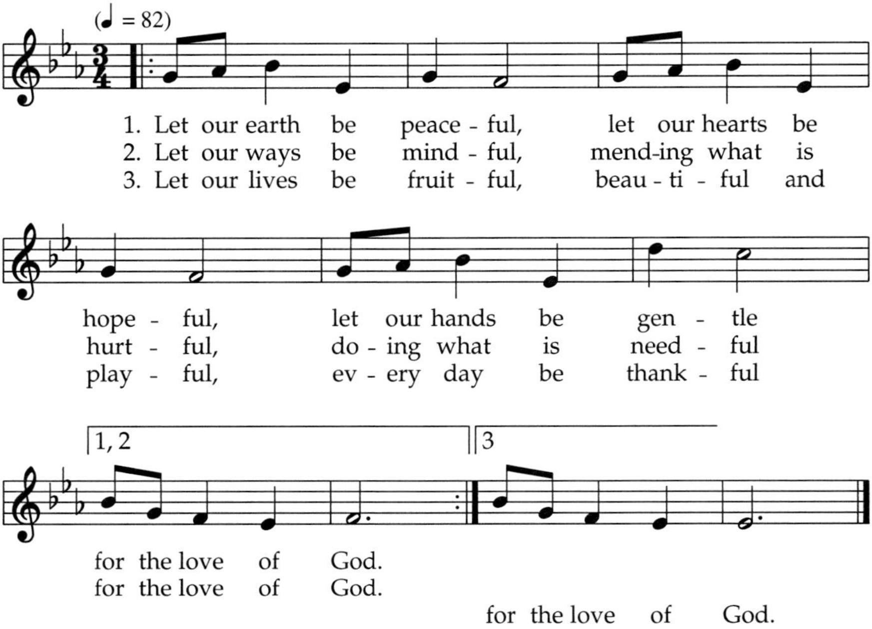

WORDS: Shirley Erena Murray
MUSIC: Carlton R. Young

RAYMOND
66.65

Here the Cross Still Casts Its Shadow

Here the cross still casts its shadow,
here we trace love's depth and height
pouring forth to bless and hallow
all who seek the holy light
that through every twist and turning
of our church's early days
helped our founders in discerning
how to serve the God they praised.

Though they long ago have parted
we today yet hold in store
gratitude for what they started
seeds of faith that grew and bore
fruit that feeds our deep attending
to the Spirit's wind and flame
and the work that God's intending
we will do in Jesus' name.

Meeting needs that stretch our mission
past the world our founders knew
yet maintaining their tradition,
Gracious God, of serving you,
while our lives keep growing, reaching,
toward the light, the love that's fed
all our praying, singing, preaching:
Christ, the church's Lord and head.

WORDS: Thomas H. Troeger

Music commissioned for the 100th anniversary of the congregation of North Broadway United Methodist Church, Columbus, Ohio, September 25, 2005

Here the Cross Still Casts Its Shadow

*Trumpet descant (stanza 3) is printed on page 33

WORDS: Thomas H. Troeger
MUSIC: Carlton R. Young

CAROL ANN
87.87 D

that through ev - ery twist and turn - ing
fruit that feeds our deep at - tend - ing
while our lives keep grow - ing, reach - ing,
of our church-'s ear - ly days helped our found-ers
to the Spir - it's wind and flame and the work that
toward the light, the love that's fed all our pray - ing,
3rd stanza rall.
resolute
in dis - cern - ing how to serve the God they praised.
God's in - tend - ing we will do in Je - sus name.
sing - ing, preach-ing: Christ the church-'s Lord and head.

Music commissioned for the 100th anniversary of the congregation of North Broadway United Methodist Church, Columbus, Ohio, September 25, 2005

Here the Cross Still Casts Its Shadow

WORDS: Thomas H. Troeger
MUSIC: Carlton R. Young

CAROL ANN
87.87 D

Music commissioned for the 100th anniversary of the congregation of North Broadway United Methodist Church, Columbus, Ohio, September 25, 2005

Here the Cross Still Casts Its Shadow

B♭ Trumpet

Play on stanza 3

(♩ = ca. 90)

MUSIC: Carlton R. Young

Out of Deep, Unordered Water

Out of deep, unordered water,
God created land and life,
world of bird and beast, and later,
twosome people, husband, wife.

Refrain
There is water in the river
bringing life to tree and plant.
Let creation praise its giver:
there is water in the font.

Refrain

Water on the human forehead,
birthmark of the love of God,
is the sign of death and rising;
through the sea there runs a road.

Refrain

Standing round the font reminds us
of the Hebrews' climb ashore.
Life is hallowed by the knowledge:
God has been this way before.

Refrain

WORDS: Fred Kaan

Out of Deep, Unordered Water

WORDS: Fred Kaan
MUSIC: Carlton R. Young

LIVING WATER
87.87 D

bird and beast, and lat - er two - some
sign of death and ris - ing; through the
hal - lowed by the knowl - edge: God has
Eb Eb Cm
peo - ple, hus - band wife.
sea there runs a road.
been this way be - fore.
Refrain
There is
F9 Bb Eb
wa - ter in the riv - er bring - ing life to tree and
Eb Eb Eb7 Ab

plant. Let cre -
Abm Abm
a - tion praise its giv - er: there is wa - ter in the
Eb Ab Eb Cm Ab
font.
1, 2 3
2. Wa - ter
3. Stand - ing
Eb Eb Eb

Out of Deep, Unordered Water

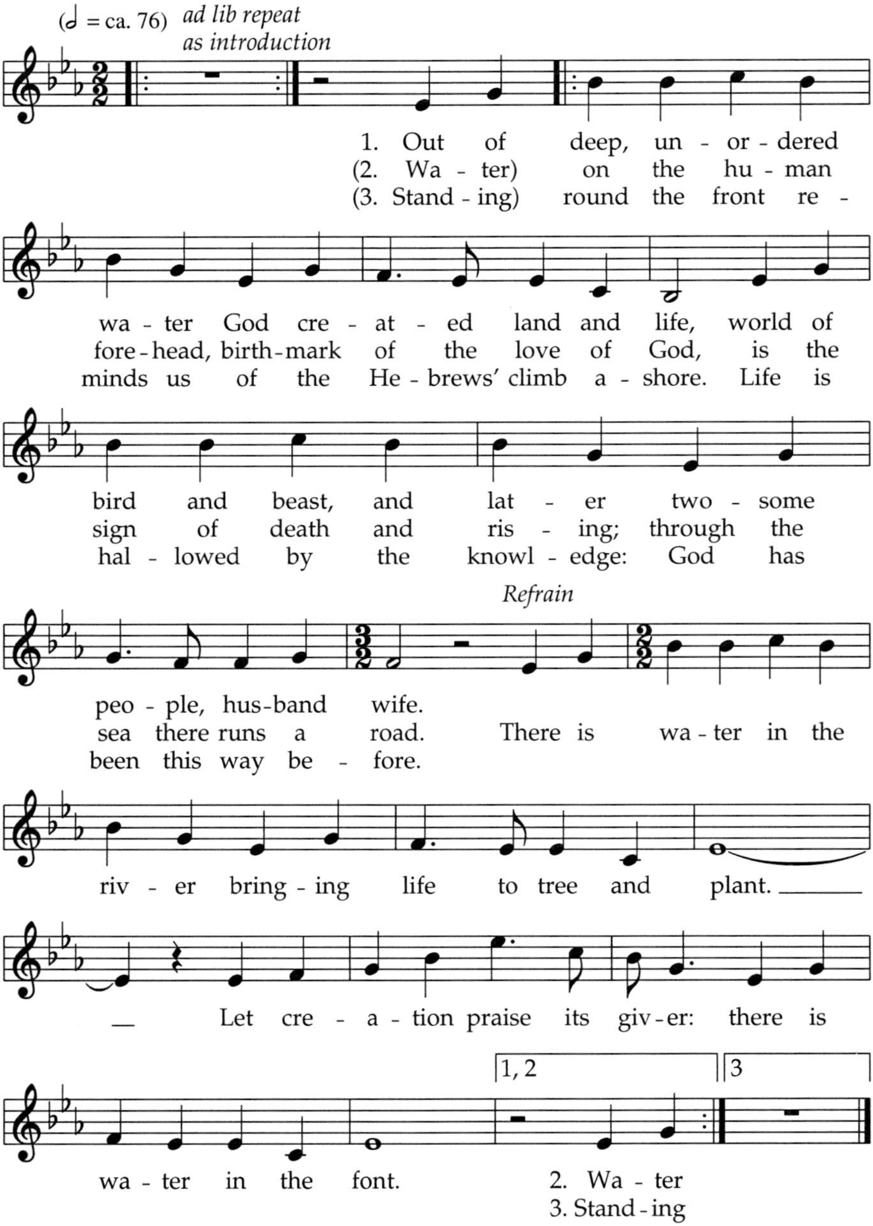

WORDS: Fred Kaan
MUSIC: Carlton R. Young

LIVING WATER
87.87 D

Be Careful

Be careful what you pray for—

you may get it!

Be careful what you sing,

for you may believe it!

Think carefully what you sing by heart,

for you may not forget it!

Think carefully what you pray by heart,

for you may receive it!

Be careful, be careful,

be careful, be careful, be careful.

WORDS: Heather Murray Elkins

For the concluding session of the Academy of Global Song
Lake Junaluska, North Carolina, October 26–29, 2003

Be Careful

WORDS: Heather Murray Elkins
MUSIC: Carlton R. Young

HEATHER
Irr.

mf
it! Think care-ful-ly what you sing by heart, for
mf
you may not for-get it! Think
care-ful-ly what you pray by heart, for

1
you may re - cieve it!
f
mp
Be
2
ceive it!
f
mp

Voice 1 mp
Voice 2
Be care - ful, be
Voice 1
Voice 2
Both
care - ful, be care - ful, be care - ful, be
care - ful.

For the concluding session of the Academy of Global Song
Lake Junaluska, North Carolina, October 26–29, 2003

Be Careful

WORDS: Heather Murray Elkins
MUSIC: Carlton R. Young

HEATHER
Irr.

When the Church of Jesus

When the church of Jesus shuts its outer door,
lest the roar of traffic drown the voice of prayer,
may our prayers, Lord, make us ten times more aware
that the world we banish is our Christian care.

If our hearts are lifted where devotion soars
high above this hungry, suffering world of ours,
lest our hymns should drug us to forget its needs,
forge our Christian worship into Christian deeds.

Lest the gifts we offer, money, talents, time,
serve to salve our conscience, to our secret shame,
Lord, reprove, inspire us by the way you give;
teach us, dying Savior, how true Christians live.

WORDS: F. Pratt Green

When the Church of Jesus

WORDS: F. Pratt Green
MUSIC: Carlton R. Young

SUTTON
65.65 D

make us ten times more a - ware
drug us to for - get its needs,
spire us by the way you give;
that the world we ban - ish is our Chris - tian
forge our Chris - tian wor - ship in - to Chris - tian
teach us, dy - ing Sav - ior,
1, 2
care.
deeds.
3
how true Chris - tians live.

When the Church of Jesus

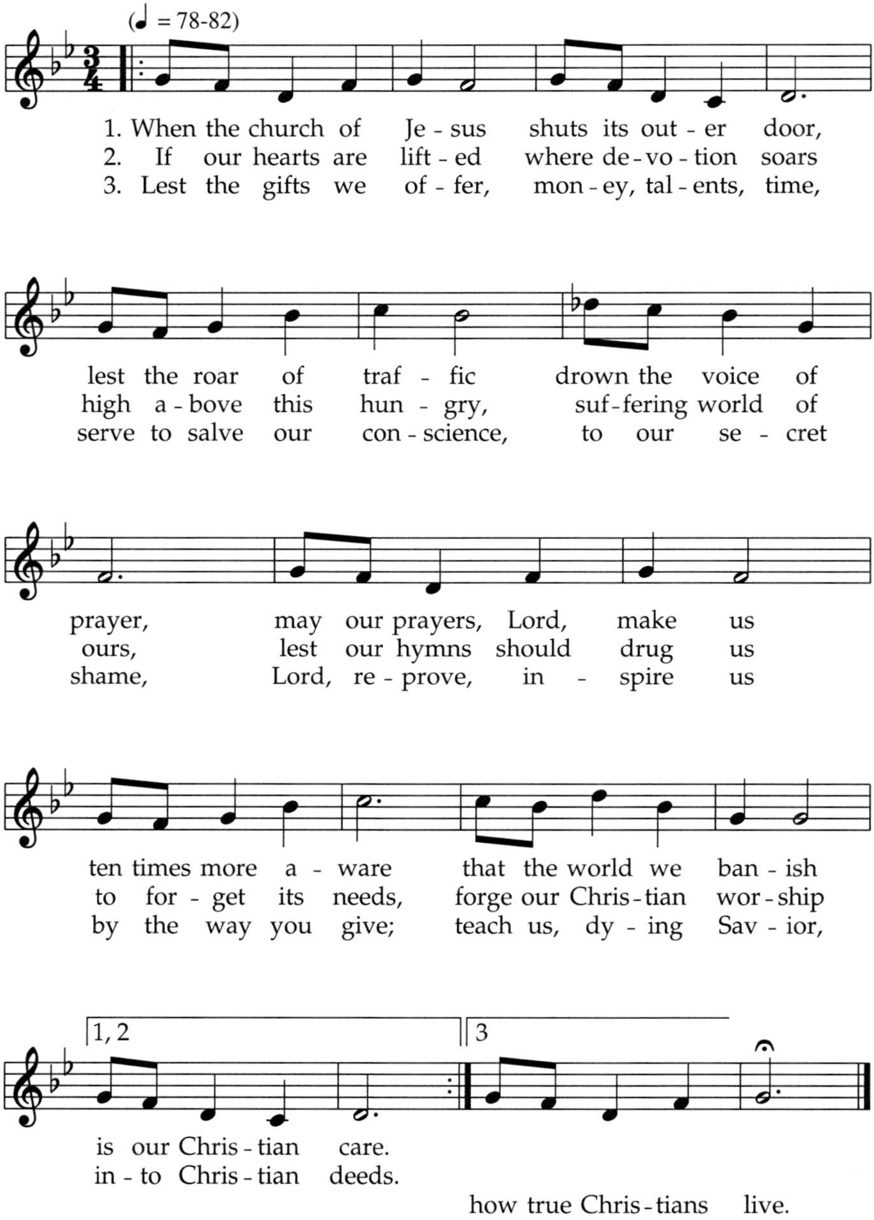

WORDS: F. Pratt Green
MUSIC: Carlton R. Young

SUTTON
65.65 D

Before a Word Was Said

Before a Word was said,
God had our ear;
before the world was made,
Jesus was here.
Ahead of Abraham,
God was, I am.

Before the Word assumed
our flesh and blood,
Jesus among us roomed
and with us stood,
Ahead of Abraham,
God was, I am.

God, Span of future, past,
our present Tense,
your Word is first and last:
eternal Sense.
Ahead of Abraham,
God was—I am—you are.

WORDS: Fred Kaan

Before a Word Was Said

WORDS: Fred Kaan
MUSIC: Carlton R. Young

TIME-WARP
10 10 10

world was made, Je - sus was here. A-head of
mong us roomed and with us stood, a-head of
first and last: e - ter - nal Sense. A-head of
A - bra-ham, God was, I am.
A - bra-ham, God was, I am.
A - bra-ham,
1, 2 rall. reflective
1, 2
rall.
sub. p
mf
3 rall.
sub. p reflective mp mf
God was — I am — you are.
3
rall.
sub. p

Before a Word Was Said

WORDS: Fred Kaan
MUSIC: Carlton R. Young

TIME-WARP
10 10 10

If Christmas Is All Red and Green

If Christmas is all red and green,
with satin bows and evergreen,
with everything exactly right,
the perfect meal and candlelight;

then Christmas is a thing we birth,
a month of stress disguised as mirth,
a time when all we know for sure:
we have to get the gift du jour.

But if there is another way,
Lord, make it plain; show us today.
Reveal your love all wrapped in flesh,
the holy child, divine largesse.

Announce once more with angel voice
that peace on earth is still your choice.

WORDS: John Thornburg

If Christmas Is All Red and Green

WORDS: John Thornburg
MUSIC: Carlton R. Young

AMOS
88.88 (+.86 st. 3)

act - ly right, the per - fect meal and can - dle -
know for sure: we have to get the gift du
wrapped in flesh, the ho - ly child, di - vine lar -
1, 2
light;
jour.
1, 2
2. then gesse.
3. But
An -
3
3

nounce once more with an - gel voice
ff
p
that
peace on earth is still your choice.

If Christmas Is All Red and Green

WORDS: John Thornburg
MUSIC: Carlton R. Young

AMOS
88.88 (+.86 st. 3)

O God of Truth and Love

O God of truth and love,
let us thy mercy prove,
bless thine ordinance divine,
let us now effectual be,
answer all its great design,
all its gracious ends in me.

O might the sacred word
set forth our dying Lord,
point us to thy sufferings past,
present grace and strength impart,
give our ravished souls a taste,
pledge of glory in our heart.

Come in thy Spirit down,
thine institution crown,
Lamb of God as slain appear,
life of all believers thou,
let us now perceive thee near,
come thou hope of glory now.

WORDS: Charles Wesley, 1745

For the World Methodist Conference, July 20–24, 2006, Seoul, Korea

O God of Truth and Love

*Percussion part is printed on page 63.

WORDS: Charles Wesley, 1745
MUSIC: Carlton R. Young

EPICLESIS
66.77.77

nance di - vine, let us now ef - fec - tual be,
suf-ferings past, pre - sent grace and strength im - part,
slain ap - pear, life of all be - liev - ers thou,
an - swer all its great de - sign, all its gra - cious
give our rav - ished souls a taste, pledge of glo - ry
let us now per - ceive thee near, come thou hope of
1, 2
ends in me.
in our heart.
glo - ry
1, 2

2. O
3. Come
3
now.
3
poco rit.

For the World Methodist Conference, July 20–24, 2006, Seoul, Korea

O God of Truth and Love

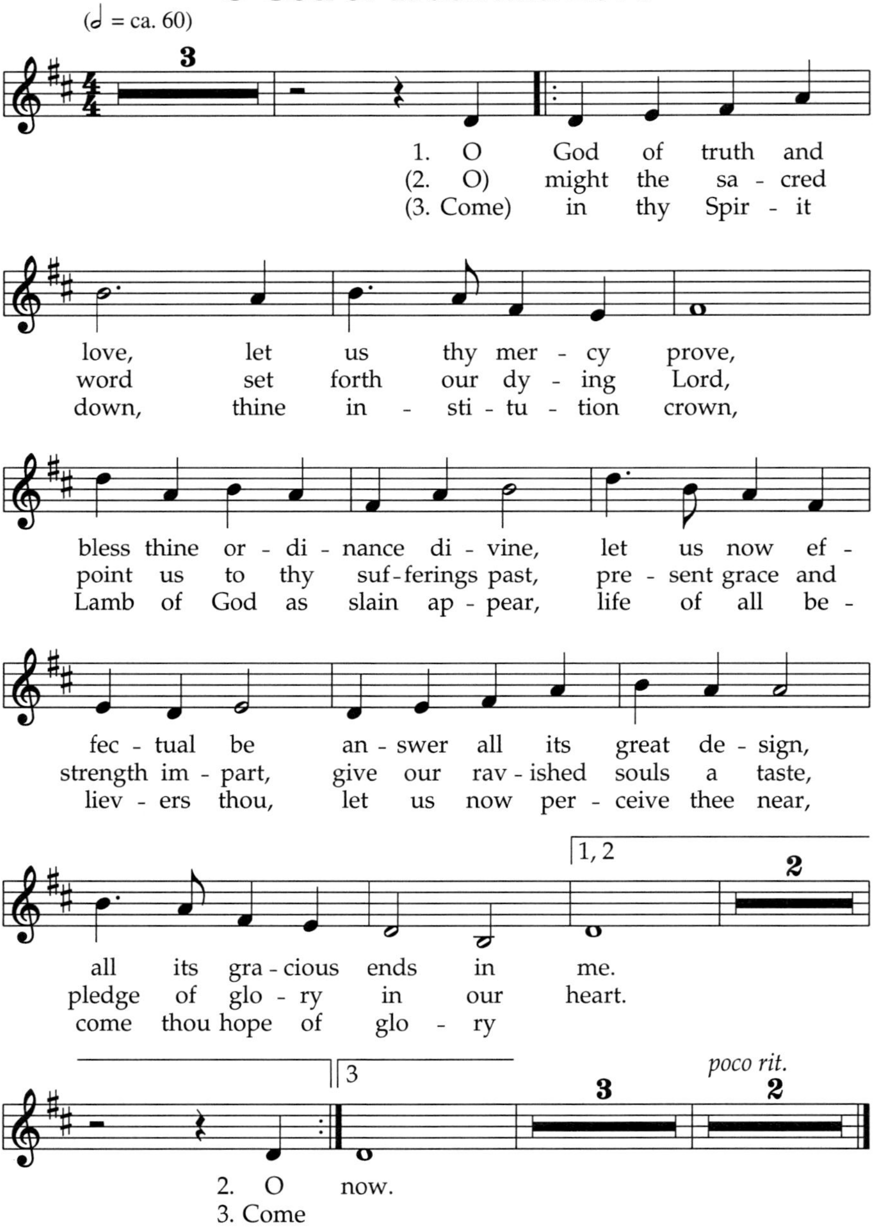

WORDS: Charles Wesley, 1745
MUSIC: Carlton R. Young

EPICLESIS
66.77.77

For the World Methodist Conference, July 20–24, 2006, Seoul, Korea

O God of Truth and Love

Percussion

MUSIC: Carlton R. Young

If You Would Hear the Angels Sing

If you would hear the angels sing
count every star at night
until your heart starts wondering
who seeds the dark with light.

For wonder is the note that sounds
when angels visit earth,
and wonder is the note that crowns
their music at Christ's birth.

Such wonder redirects our sight
from all the stars above
to find that heaven's brightest light
shines here on earth as love.

WORDS: Thomas Troeger

For Polly Brecht

If You Would Hear the Angels Sing

Calypso (♩ = 138)

*A percussion part is found on page 69.
**Appoggiaturas are played on the beat.

WORDS: Thomas Troeger
MUSIC: Carlton R. Young

POLLY
CM

an - gels sing count ev - ery star at night un -
note that sounds when an - gels vis - it earth, and
rects our sight from all the stars a - bove to
Claps
til your heart starts won - der - ing who seeds the dark
won - der is the note that crowns their mu - sic at
find that heav - en's bright - est light shines here on earth
(-Perc.)
1, 2
with light.
Christ's birth.
as
1, 2
(+Perc.)

mp
3
2. For
3. Such
love.
3
(+Perc.)
love.
love.
Claps
ff

For Polly Brecht

If You Would Hear the Angels Sing

WORDS: Thomas Troeger
MUSIC: Carlton R. Young

POLLY
CM

For Polly Brecht

If You Would Hear the Angels Sing

Percussion

Calypso (♩ = 138)

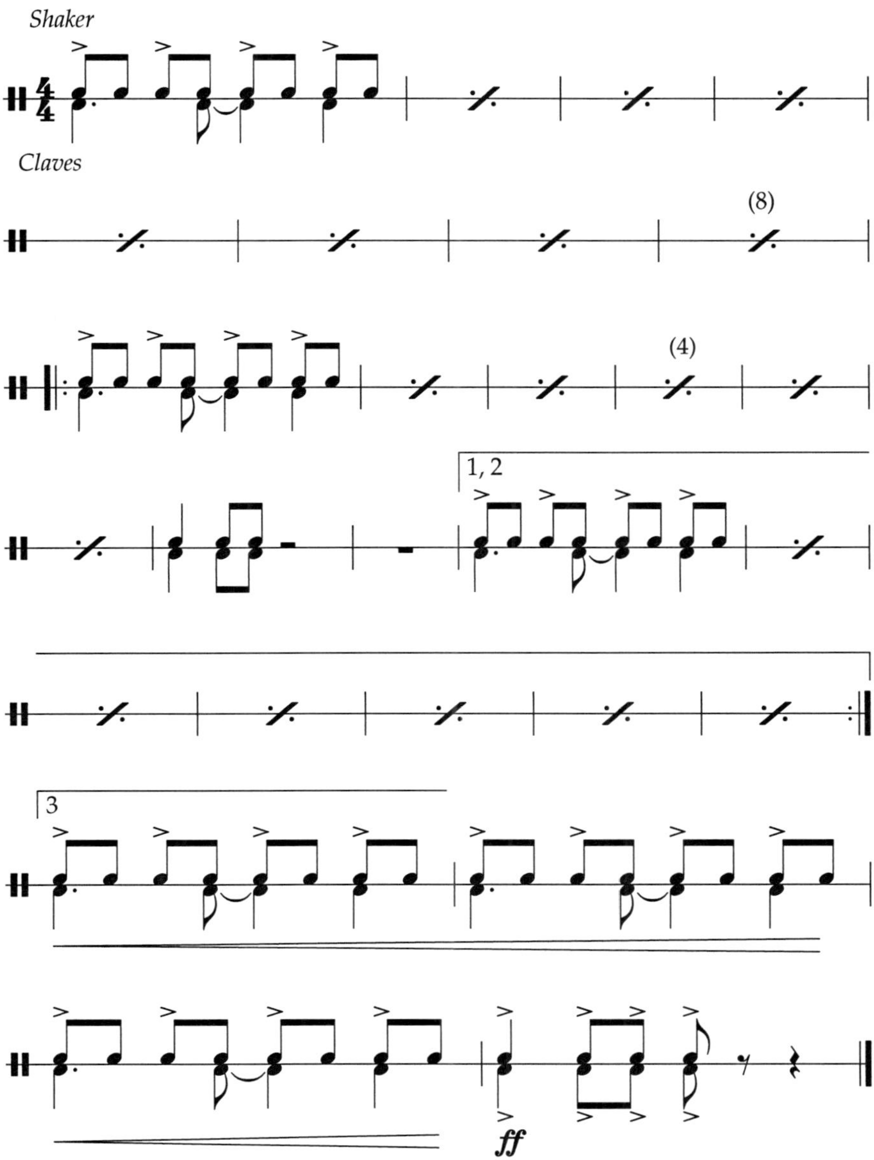

MUSIC: Carlton R. Young

Jesus, United By Thy Grace

Jesus, united by our grace
and each to each endeared,
with confidence we seek thy face
and know our prayer is heard.

Help us to help each other, Lord,
each other's cross to bear;
let all their friendly aid afford,
and feel each other's care.

Up unto thee, our living Head,
let us in all things grow;
till you have made us free indeed
and spotless here below.

Touched by the lodestone of thy love,
let all our hearts agree,
and ever toward each other move,
and ever move toward thee.

To thee, inseparably joined,
let all our spirits cleave;
O may we all the loving mind
that was in thee receive.

This is the bond of perfectness,
thy spotless charity;
O let us, still we pray, possess
the mind that was in thee.

WORDS: Charles Wesley, 1742

For S T Kimbrough, Jr., on his retirement from
The General Board of Global Ministries: The United Methodist Church, June 6, 2006

Jesus, United By Thy Grace

WORDS: Charles Wesley, 1742
MUSIC: Carlton R. Young

VERSTAND VON CHRIST
CM

deared, with con - fi -
bear; let all their
grow; till you have
gree, and ev - er
cleave; O may we
ty; O let us,
dence we seek thy face and
friend - ly aid af - ford, and
made us free in - deed and
toward each oth - er move, and
all the lov - ing mind that
still we pray, pos - sess the

1–5
know our prayer is heard.
feel each oth - er's care.
spot - less here be - low.
ev - er move toward thee.
was in thee re - ceive.
mind that was in
1–5
thee.
6
6 8va
loco
In
thee, in thee, in thee.

For S T Kimbrough, Jr., on his retirement from
The General Board of Global Ministries: The United Methodist Church, June 6, 2006

Jesus, United By Thy Grace

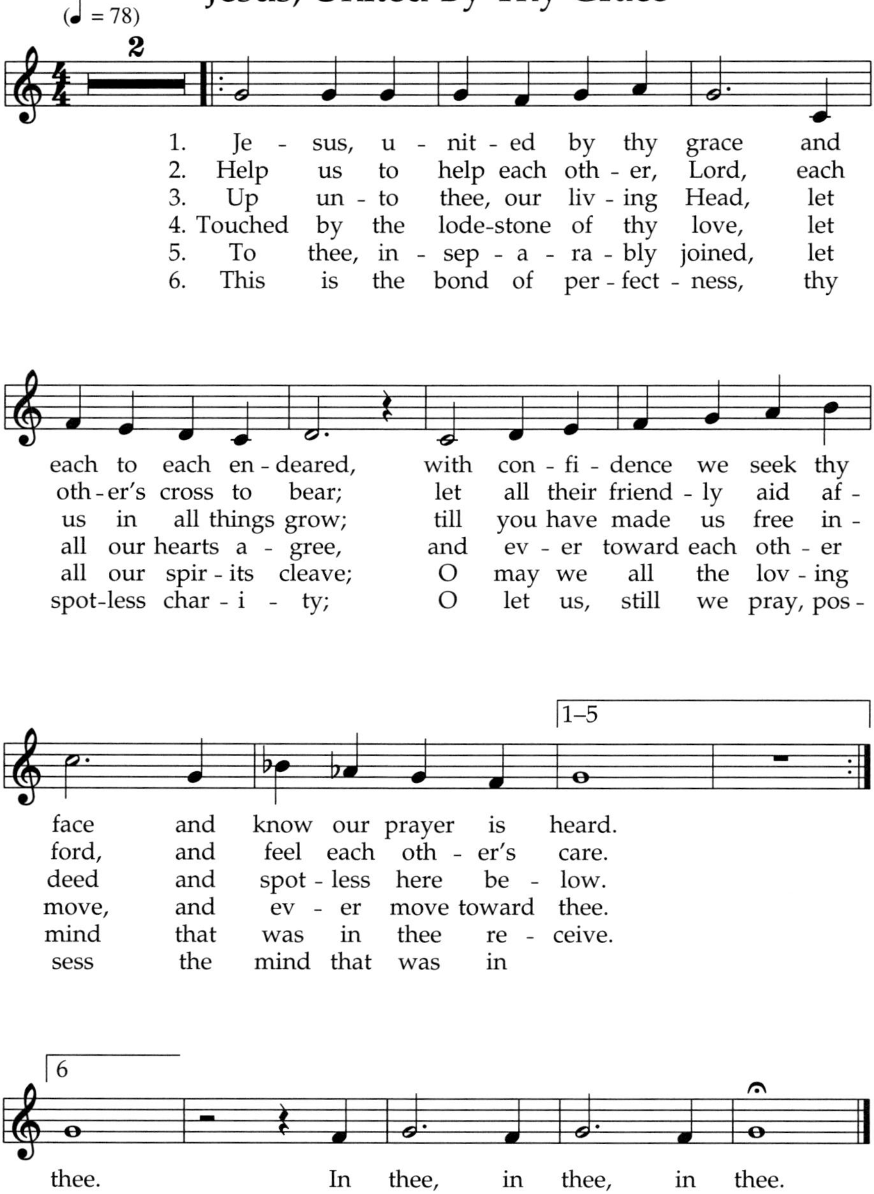

WORDS: Charles Wesley, 1742
MUSIC: Carlton R. Young

VERSTAND VON CHRIST
CM

God, Give Me Time to Learn the Words

God, give me time to learn the words
I find so hard to say:
the loving words, forgiving words
that take the sting away;
God, give me calm to ride the storm
when waves of anger rise,
a moment when I see the truth
my lesser self denies.

God, give me time to deal with words
that threaten and destroy,
the easy words of politics
that kill creation's joy;
speeches that will proliferate
economies of greed,
the thieves of children's heritage,
the poison in the seed.

God, give me time to heed the words
that history forgot,
that clear the air for doves to fly,
that loose the deadly knot:
love that the caring Spirit brings
more potent than the law,
with mercy wiping debt away
and closing hunger's maw.

God, give us time to grasp your Word,
transforming as we go
our little worlds, our larger worlds
by all we do and know,
finding in one another's faith
the wisdom and the grace
that Jesus Christ was born to bring
and gave a human face.

WORDS: Shirley Erena Murray

God, Give Me Time to Learn the Words

WORDS: Shirley Erena Murray
MUSIC: Carlton R. Young

GOTTES ZEIT
CMD

God, give me calm to ride the storm when waves of an - ger
speech - es that will pro - lif - er - ate e - con - o - mies of
love that the car - ing Spir - it brings more po - tent then the
find - ing in one an - oth - er's faith the wis - dom and the
rise, a mo - ment when I see the truth my
greed, the thieves of chil - dren's her - i - tage, the
law, with mer - cy wip - ing debt a - way and
grace that Je - sus Christ was born to bring and
1–3
4
less - er self de - nies.
poi - son in the seed.
clos - ing hun - ger's maw.
gave a hu - man face.

God, Give Me Time to Learn the Words

WORDS: Shirley Erena Murray
MUSIC: Carlton R. Young

GOTTES ZEIT
CMD

Now As We Go

Now as we go, kind Spirit keep us,
in all we see, be Christ our focus,
in all we do, his story shape us,
that we may grow to God's good purpose.

Now as we go, as sister and brother,
give us good care of one another,
more hope to share, more strength to gather,
more life to know in faith together.

Amen. Amen.
Amen. Amen.

WORDS: Shirley Erena Murray

For the banquet honoring Don E. Saliers,
"Worship Comes to Life," Candler School of Theology, Emory University, October 11, 2005

Now As We Go

WORDS: Shirley Erena Murray
MUSIC: Carlton R. Young

HONORAND
99.99. with Amen

that we may grow to God's good pur-pose.
more life to know in faith to - geth-er.
A - men. A - men.
rit. on repeat
A - men. A - men. men.
rit. on repeat

For the banquet honoring Don E. Saliers,
"Worship Comes to Life," Candler School of Theology, Emory University, October 11, 2005

Now As We Go

WORDS: Shirley Erena Murray
MUSIC: Carlton R. Young

HONORAND
99.99. with Amen

We Lift Our Hearts to You

We lift our hearts to you,
O Daystar from on high!
The sun itself is but your shade,
yet cheers both earth and sky.

O let your orient beams
the night of sin disperse,
the mists of error and of vice
that shade the universe.

How beauteous nature now!
How stark and sad before!
With joy we view the pleasing change,
and nature's God adore.

May we this life improve,
to mourn for errors past,
and live this short revolving day
as if it were our last.

To God: Creator, Son,
and Spirit, One-in-three,
be glory; as it was, is now,
and shall forever be,
and shall forever be,
and shall forever be,
and shall forever be.

WORDS: Attr. to John Wesley, 1741, alt.

for Russell E. Richey

We Lift Our Hearts to You

*Opt. Bass, Drums, and Tambourine (ad lib)

WORDS: Attr. to John Wesley, 1741, alt.
MUSIC: Carlton R. Young

RICHEY
SM

The sun it - self is but your shade, yet cheers both earth and sky.
the mists of er - ror and of vice that shade the u - ni-verse.
With joy we view the pleas-ing change, and na - ture's God a - dore.
and live this short re - volv-ing day as if it were our last.
be glo - ry; as it was, is now, and shall for - ev - er be,
2. O
3. How
4. May
5. To
1–4
5
and shall for - ev - er be, and
N.C. C9 F F9/A B♭ F/A Gm7(♭5)
F/C C7(♭9) F N.C. C
N.C. C F2 F B♭m6/D♭ B♭m6 F/C N.C. Gm7(♭5)

shall for - ev - er be, and
F2/C F C7(♭9) F N.C. B♭m/D♭
shall for - ev - er
F/C D♭7(♯5) Gm7(♭5) F/C Csus
be.
F N.C. C13sus

for Russell E. Richey

We Lift Our Hearts to You

WORDS: Attr. to John Wesley, 1741, alt.
MUSIC: Carlton R. Young

RICHEY
SM

Notes

These performance notes are offered in addition to tempo, dynamic, and performance instructions in the music. The whole group need not sing all stanzas. Hymns may be sung antiphonally—for example, male/female or solo/soli voices on selected stanzas.

1. "We Are One in Christ," a song of Christian unity and reconciliation, was composed for United Methodist Bishop Sally Dyck. It was sung in the fall of 2004 in the departing service at the church where she was pastor, Garfield Memorial United Methodist Church, Pepper Pike, Ohio, and at her several installation/reception services in the Minnesota area of The United Methodist Church.
2. "Lord, We Have Your Commission" was written during a missions leadership training event, and the musical setting (with apologies to S. S. Wesley) was composed shortly thereafter.
3. "Take a Tune" elaborates Erik Routley's famous description of church musicians: "who handle mysteries and make them friendly."
5. "Let Our Earth Be Peaceful" is both a plea to God's family to be more human and responsible for God's creation, and a prayer of thanksgiving for God's sustaining love. RAYMOND is the composer's grandson, who is autistic.
7. This boom-chunk setting of Fred Kaan's baptismal hymn, "Out of Deep, Unordered Water," commemorates his visit to Nashville and attending the Grand Old Opry. The last two lines of the refrain may be sung or played ad lib between stanzas or as a coda.
9. This setting of Fred Pratt Green's classic hymn about the social responsibilities of urban churches, "When the Church of Jesus Shuts Its Outer Door," was commissioned by the late Bernard Braley for the poet's memorial service, June 2, 2002, at Wesley Chapel, City Road, London.
10. "Before a Word Was Said" is a thoughtful, lyrical exegesis of John 8:58, "Before Abraham was, I am." The musical setting moves toward and away from those words; and the ending "God was, I am, you are," is unresolved on a dominant chord.
11. In performing this fresh and playful "If Christmas Is All Red and Green," a flute may double the right hand in the introduction and the endings, and *pizzicato* cello and/or string bass may double the left hand.
12. "O God of Truth and Love" should be accompanied by piano, Korean drum, and a suspended cymbal. A large Chinese gong is struck on the last beat, and left to vibrate.
15. Play/sing "God, Give Me Time to Learn the Words" in a leisurely blues style.
17. "We Lift Our Hearts to You," dedicated to Russell E. Richey, Wesleyan scholar and former Dean of Candler School of Theology, Emory University, may also be sung as a choral call to worship, or as a choir processional.

Metrical Index

Topical Index